For information about permission to reproduce excerpts from this book write to:
Derek O'Neill
244 5th Avenue, Suite D-264
New York, NY 10001
E-Mail: info@derekoneill.com

ISBN: 978-1-936470-32-7
First Edition

Get a Grip Series © 2013
Editor: Nancy Moss
Front Cover Design: © 2013 by Derek O'Neill and Cléa Owens

DEDICATION

To all who read this book, I salute you for wanting to change the way you live for the better and for having the courage to be who you are as fully as possible.

To all who encourage me everyday to keep going and sharing their lives with me, family small and large. But most of all the little angel who came to teach me – Alexa, my granddaughter.

"Everybody hurts sometimes, and when we do it is nice to have Derek O'Neill around. His excellent little books on the things that get us, (fear, anger, depression, victimhood, mental blocks) allow us to find our way safely through our psychological minefields and arrive safely at the other side. Read them when you need them."

Paul Perry, Author of the
New York Times Bestseller
Evidence of the Afterlife

TABLE OF CONTENTS

Author's Preface ix

What Does Abundance Really Mean? 1

The State Of Lack – Scarcity Mentality vs. Abundance Mentality 7

Manifesting The Power of Creation 13

The Courage To Be Authentic – Are You Able to Receive? 19

Your Inner Voice – Self-Talk, Self-Worth and Letting Go of Anger 25

Eliminating What You Don't Need - What Is Truly Important to You 31

Giving and Service – The Way to Abundance 35

Abundance and Mindfulness 38

Exercises/Meditations on Abundance 41

AUTHOR'S PREFACE

Thank you for purchasing *Abundance – Starts Right Now.* This book has not come about as a result of my training as a therapist, but through some hard-earned lessons that I have experienced myself. This is how I know the path out of limiting beliefs and behaviors that hinder growth. The tools that I offer in this book have worked not only for me, but also for hundreds if not thousands of other people. I have shared these ideas and techniques in my workshops, one-on-one sessions, video and radio broadcasts, and on my website, and I have witnessed astounding results time and time again. Through observation of others, and myself, I have learned to identify the triggers and root causes of disharmony. Most of all, I have come to understand and apply the best methods for achieving peace and balance in life; not perfection, but real transformation and harmony that comes with learning who we are and what makes us tick. My 35 years of martial arts study has given me a refined sense of timing for when to strike with the sword to cut away old patterns, and when to use the brush to paint the picture of the life we deserve and can have.

The 'Get a Grip' series of books offers tangible, authentic wisdom that can help you in all aspects of your life. You've made a great choice by investing in this book. Enjoy the read, and take time to learn and apply the techniques. Let's change who we are together.

- Derek

Abundance

starts right now

WHAT DOES ABUNDANCE REALLY MEAN?

The word "abundance" is a big word, not necessarily in length, but certainly in meaning. What is the first thing you think when you hear "abundance?" Money? Love? A large circle of friends and family? While we can apply the concept of abundance to all of those aspects of our lives, the essential meaning of abundance is that you are solidly happy with who you are and no external event or situation – whether good or bad – can add or subtract from that happiness. No one is happy all the time, but when you are truly in a mindset of abundance, you live with balance, hopefulness and unlimited possibility. Our innate nature is one of peace and abundance; it comes from within.

Abundance is a way of thinking and of living, even when you have less money, love or support than you would like. Life delivers a continually changing set of circumstances. Living in abundance can give you a constant source of stability that isn't based on external things, but you must change your perspective and believe in all the potential that lies within your reach. Abundance is a state of mind. Abundance can't be lost, taken or bestowed on you. It is about what brings you joy and fulfillment, not about what you have. The pursuit of "more," which is so common in our culture, is not the road to abundance.

Money can no doubt make life easier, but it does not buy happiness, as the saying goes. The obsessive pursuit of money can create an imbalance that stands in the way of the kind of abundance that is genuine. If you focus too narrowly on having more money, deeper love, or a wildly successful career, and become convinced that those things will "fix" everything, you'll lose sight of the bigger picture of abundance. Abundance that concentrates on one thing is destined to create discontent and disappointment. You must look at every aspect of your life. When I studied anatomy and physiology, years ago as a fitness instructor, I came to learn that you couldn't lose weight or gain muscle on just one part of your body. Doing crunches to develop a six-pack won't work unless you tone up everything else! Think of abundance the same way. Pursuing money without bringing the consciousness of abundance to everything in your life will be a fleeting and empty experience. Everything is connected to everything else, so just making loads of money, or finding love, won't bring you abundance in the true sense of the word.

The opposite and mirror image of abundance is lack. Both have more to do with your point of view - not the amount of money, love or happiness that you have, or don't have. "Lack" doesn't mean that you don't have enough of something. It is a negative way of thinking that keeps people from their full potential. Lack is the mentality that there's a shortage or scarcity of good things in life, and then you create fear around that idea. Operating from a place of lack skews the truth of abundance in life and colors your perspective toward hopelessness and futility. To understand abundance, and how it can be yours, you have to grasp how the mindset of lack may be playing a role in your life.

We all act from our consciousness, whatever it is at any given moment. What is the consciousness of abundance? What is the consciousness of lack? We draw in the elements that reflect our consciousness. When you are operating from a place of abundance, you gather more abundance. The same is true of lack. Thoughts that are familiar and comfortable tend to dominate your experience, no matter how much you want to affect change in your life. Fear is the root cause of lack consciousness. Think about how fear may be blocking your potential by holding you hostage in the feeling of defeat, before you even begin.

I have found, over the years, that more people fear success than fear failure. I've watched them sabotage themselves while climbing up their careers ladders. In fact, I did the same thing in my own early adulthood. I'd always get to the top and then do something to interfere with my progress. I began to notice this pattern, and finally realized that I would always get bored with success. (I get bored very easily!) I needed to be of service to tap into the true feeling of abundance. Now, I'm always looking for new ways to help people. I cherish the gift of giving to others.

Authentic abundance comes when you have balanced everything in your life, as best as you can. That includes giving away what you have too much of. If you have a lot of love but not enough money, what should you give away? Love. Do you have more money than some other things in life? Give away some money! Money is blocked by fear. It takes courage and love to give AND to receive. It is all about balance. The things that you want in your life, you must first give away. If you give more hugs, you will get more kisses! You have to break the fear – that is what is causing the lack. Self-sabotage happens when you have too much of something and you become complacent, disconnected, and sometimes even greedy.

In the pages that follow, it is my hope that you'll find the key to unlock the negative mindsets, misguided resignation, and past hurts, all of which might be impeding abundance. When you look at abundance with new meaning, and discover it inside yourself, there's no limitation on the extraordinary life that you can experience.

THE STATE OF LACK – SCARCITY MENTALITY VS. ABUNDANCE MENTALITY

It is important to understand the difference between abundance mentality, and a scarcity mentality. If you adopt an abundance mentality, the lens through which you see the world is much clearer and brighter. Though you may find it difficult to summon up the idea that there is unlimited possibility for you in the world, especially when you are facing huge challenges, the alternative - to live with a scarcity mentality - will only produce more anxiety and feelings of low self-esteem. Thinking you don't have enough becomes equated with the feeling that YOU are "not enough."

How can you climb up into abundance when you have created a wall of fear and defeat around yourself? There are people with plenty of money who have scarcity mentality. We live in a culture that pressures us to grab what we can, fill up our houses with stuff we don't need, compete with our neighbor for a piece of the pie, and measure our personal worth by a bank account, a slim body, or a powerful job. Some people take on those misguided paths to happiness and let them rule their lives. Under the surface of that sensibility is someone who is living in fear, unable to really enjoy all that they have.

Your mind is speaking to you continuously. Abundance mentality is the voice in your head that says there is opportunity for you, that you can always start fresh, and that there are as many chances for change as there are days in your life. You may think that looking at the world with abundance mentality is avoiding the truth of suffering and real, sometimes insurmountable, problems. In fact, embracing abundance is recognition of reality - the good, the bad and everything in-between. It is the abundance of experience, the abundance of situations, the abundance of human possibility. You can't affect real transformation in your life, or the lives of others who need help, from a mentality of scarcity. If you operate from a state of lack, you only see the complications and barriers. Well, no doubt, there are heavy obstacles out there, but so many of them can be moved if you start from a consciousness of abundance!

It would be foolish to say that the mentality of scarcity is easy to keep at bay. Our society pushes the idea that we need more and that once you have more, you'll be happy. Though natural resources diminish by humankind's overuse and waste, the natural resources that reside in our minds are boundless. Does that mean we don't get caught up feeling lack, at times? Of course not, but when you can shift that view and come back to abundance, you can eventually learn to stay there more often. The panic and fear caused by the belief that you will not get something you need or want can shut down a healthy perspective. It is like pulling down the blinds in a room and forgetting that there is a whole wide world out there. If you create an environment of anxiety, and sit down in the middle of it with your eyes closed, it is obvious that those negative feelings will only grow. It is going to get harder and harder to find the door out of that room unless you see some light shining under it!

You have to be open to abundance. An abundant life doesn't magically happen by shifting your perspective, but what does happen is that you begin to notice good things and see the possibilities around you. When you're in a scarcity mentality you miss them. Once you notice abundance, it starts connecting in your life. You act on making things happen for yourself and you find a path to follow to get where you want to go. If you live under a cloud of lack, you might give up on yourself before you've even tried.

Gratitude plays a big role in the scarcity mentality vs. abundance mentality tussle of the mind. Think about what you are grateful for, and go beyond the obvious examples. Of course you cherish your family, the roof over your head, and the food on your plate, but what else? How about the qualities that you embody? The small moments between you and your child or a pet? The deep green of that lush tree outside of your window? Surround yourself with abundance and try to spend time with people who are also in that mindset. The mentality of scarcity can drag you down, and at times, be downright toxic. It may also be helpful to think about painful experiences and the messages you got from family in the past that may be coloring what is good in your present life.

Process those feelings, and then let them go. The syndrome of "not enough" is a vicious cycle that detracts from the true meaning of abundance.

When our finances are precarious, or we desperately want someone to love, or we feel we can't get the acknowledgment we deserve, remember that situations will usually shift over time, and then shift again. You have to defuse and deflate your fear and panic. They are trying hard to distract you from your own truth – that change is not only possible, but also probable. The journey you are on might not be comfortable, but hitting bottom in any aspect of your life may be the only way to rise again. Failure could be the best thing that ever happened to you. If you dread it, you won't be able to partake in its hidden gift. Living becomes less about struggle and more about the richness of experience.

MANIFESTING THE POWER OF CREATION

We hear a lot about manifesting abundance. It sounds good, but what does it really mean? Beyond the cliché of conjuring up money, manifestation is based on the absolute truth that each and every one of us is forming our own reality. Think of it as the Power of Creation, which is a simple idea that says that if you put your mind to something you can manifest it. The problem for most people is the struggle between the conscious mind and the unconscious mind. The very powerful unconscious mind usually wins! The result can be what people call failure. They say they tried and failed, but did they feel on some level that they were going to fail even before they started? Did they give any time to thinking about what they were going to manifest? A rush to acquire wealth or happiness can lead to a lot of suffering when things don't work out as we imagined. This can happen even when we achieve the trappings of money or whatever it is that we thought would fix everything.

You need to sit with yourself, slow down, and go deeper instead of jumping into manifesting. You will find that your manifestations will have a lesson for you, as you discover who you really are and what is important to you. There's a misconception that in order to heal another, you have to be healed. You do not have to be "fixed" in order to help somebody else – you just have to be "real." We all have things we are good at, and when we help one another, in whatever way we can, there's true manifestation of exchange. It is helpful to remember that you are succeeding on your journey, no matter how things may appear. You may not understand why you have manifested something that seems contrary to what you want, but you have created it for a reason.

When we use the power of manifestation consciously, it is sometimes much easier when we are doing it for somebody else. You might very well be able to raise money for charity, but not be able to pay your mortgage. Why is that? You can be very powerful in creating abundance when you are doing it for somebody else, but your self-worth is blocked. Look at the areas of your life where you create abundance, and the parts of your life where you are blocked. Once you understand that you are responsible for everything you manifest, you'll stop blaming others. Your energy is severely drained for manifesting abundance when you fault other people. Most importantly, accept that everything that you are manifesting is presenting itself not to hurt you, but to enlighten you. When you understand that, life becomes more precious, beautiful, and abundant. You realize how powerful and deserving you really are.

If as individuals we are creating all this substance in our lives, can you imagine how much more powerful it gets if a community clicks in to the same consciousness, whether it be positive or negative? When economic shakeups happen across the globe, scare mongering that there is no money is a common phenomenon. Usually there's still a lot of money floating around, but people who have it are affected by the propaganda, and they hold on tight to their cash and investments. That is when economies slow and positive thinking fades. In our own lives, it is a symbolic reflection of slowing and blocking the life force that should be flowing through us. Everything comes with a message; whether it is an illness, or a challenge, or a disappointment. That message is telling you that something you're doing is out of alignment with your highest good. When you say, "I have a pain in my neck," go back one hour in your life, and ask, "Who have I been talking to?" or "Where have I been?" I guarantee you will find out what the pain in the neck is all about! It is always connected to an interaction that has manifested for your enlightenment. Everything that you manifest is a window into who you are at that point in your life.

When we look at abundance from a worldview, we need to be more aware of what humankind is thinking about, what we are giving our attention to, and what we want to change. If people start thinking more positively again, we are going to see transformation, first at a very subtle level, but then it will grow. When you are very fearful about losing what you have, or not getting what you need, you may feel that positive thinking cannot help. That is a guaranteed way to block abundance. You'll close down and live in that mentality of scarcity where nothing is truly satisfying. Manifesting abundance is about courage to connect with all the riches inside you, and the relationship and responsibility that you have to others. We can create a mentality of abundance in our homes, our communities and our world.

Attitude constructs our reality. Living in the moment can help to focus attitude. Instead of worrying about tomorrow, or what wrongs were done to you in the past, when you are in the here and now, it is much easier to have a positive, aligned attitude of happiness and contentment. You place a wedge between you and abundance when you think about what you don't have, instead of what you want. And if you focus too narrowly, and not look at the bigger picture of abundance, you'll miss all the universe has to offer. A positive attitude is about connecting every part of you - your head, your heart, and your hands, which can reach out to others – into one fluid state if being.

THE COURAGE TO BE AUTHENTIC – ARE YOU ABLE TO RECEIVE?

The universe cannot respond to you until you learn its language. What is the universe saying to us? It is saying that there is plenty of everything for everybody. If you don't embrace that message, you cannot receive. There is a joke that illustrates that idea beautifully: A man dies, and he goes to heaven, where he meets St. Peter at the gate. Peter looks over the list for the man's name and he says, "I don't see your name here. Let me just go in and check with the boss. Go to that room over there and take a seat." When the man opens the door to the room, he finds a massive space filled with yachts, houses, cars, swimming pools, people — everything you could ever think of. The man shuts the door, then goes to a chair and sits down. Peter calls the man over and says, "Well, there, yep, you're on my list, come on in. Do you have you any questions?" The man asks, "Why are there all kinds of things in that room over there? What is that about?" Peter replies, "Oh, that's all the stuff that people asked for, and were given, but they were not able to receive them."

How do you learn to receive? If you are stuck in a state of lack of abundance, it is because your mind is telling you that you're not worthy enough. It could be the programming and messaging you received as a child, or something that is going on in your life that reinforces a false self-image for you. We can't erase all of this with a wave of our arm, but what we can do is surrender. I don't mean surrender as in giving up or becoming lazy. Surrender in this context means saying to yourself, "I do everything I can with what I have." When you want to give and receive, you find a way. Perhaps you discover that the feeling of not deserving good things in your life stems from one or both of your parents implanting that message when you were a child. It is by surrendering, letting go of blame, and focusing on what you can do in this moment that will open you to new perspectives. You may not be aware of how you hinder your ability to receive, since that block can lie deep in your subconscious.

If you want abundance, the worst thing you can do is to assume the misguided conviction that you are somehow unlucky or different than someone who achieves everything they want. There are situations that can make one person's path seemingly easier than others, but the truth is that underneath any definition you may feel confined by, lays your authentic self. What are you good at? Who are you meant to be, regardless of your circumstances? The journey to meaningful and lasting abundance starts there.

We live in a world of cause and effect. What you sow is what you reap. Sooner or later what you give out has to come back. If you trust yourself enough to be authentic, and give and receive with a genuine heart, the universe responds with the same authenticity and sends it back to you. Trust is about the self. When you find yourself not knowing how to trust your true self, it is probably connected to something that was said in your childhood. It is up to you to say, "Well, I'm an adult now, so those experiences don't have to be the same. I can change them." That requires the courage to look at parts of you that may be wounded, instead of trying to push them away. It is important to acknowledge, and even thank, those damaged aspects of yourself for informing you, and giving you the experience. That is when you can heal and trust in abundance.

The love versus fear factor is part of the quest to live in abundance. Our authentic state is love. Fear is not unnatural, it is inherent in our reactions and emotions, but that doesn't make it real. Love flows and fear struggles; try to catch those fearful moments. Have a conversation with them. Are they based on reality, or are you angry, worried, sad, even hungry or tired? The authentic self is attuned to self-care. Observe how when you feel fear there is tightness inside of you. You can almost literally feel a wall going up between you and the world. Think about love and take that wall down. You cannot connect with the world, and the abundance of the world, when you live behind a wall of fear.

We know the concept of "fear of success," but what is underneath that idea and how can we change it? There is a lot of evidence that, after your basic needs are met, money has no correlation to happiness. People with lots of extra money in the bank – even if they are billionaires - are not happier than people who don't have a lot. Society programs you to think differently. Let's look more closely at the idea of succeeding and success being two separate things. Success, defined by our culture, tends to be connected to wealth and power, but wouldn't you say that someone who is happy and fulfilled, no matter what is in their bank account, is succeeding in life?

If you turn the word around to define what is truly important to you, "success," and whatever that means to you, can be attainable. What are your associations with success? Are they negative because of someone in your life who had a lot of success disappointed you on a personal level? Do you think of people with money as not being well liked? Were you told you wouldn't be successful, that your ideas or dreams were silly or impractical? When you tap into the authentic self, you begin to do what you want to do, and form your own opinions. Yes, we all have to do some things that we prefer not to, but if you can embrace what you want the majority of the time, you'll see how powerful you are. So many people feel confined by the box they feel they've been put in – but you have the key to release yourself!

YOUR INNER VOICE – SELF-TALK, SELF-WORTH AND LETTING GO OF ANGER

Your mind listens to everything that you say. It will manifest whatever it is - good, bad or anything in-between - in vast amounts. In other words, if you have a mentality of abundance, you will have an abundance of it! The same is true for living in fear and a state of lack. That fear will feed on itself, as your mind is incredibly powerful. What you say to your mind, "such as" or "including" positive affirmations is important to shift your perspective away from a mentality of scarcity.

You may know the teaching that states, "In the beginning there was the Word," and that the Word is what brings us to being human. Our lives are manifest by words, and the words in your mind are what your consciousness is powered by. Everything starts with a single thought. The sequence of those thoughts is what makes the difference on how you manifest what you want.

Here's a technique to begin creating a connection between words and affecting change in your life: Start with a thought, and then speak it out loud. For example, "I would like to meet people who can help me on my path to find a new job." Don't keep the thought in your head. The vibrations of words are very powerful. When you speak them out loud the energy of the Universe conspires to bring about manifestation. Will these words magically bring what you want to your door? No - you have to go into action and have a plan, which is your way of meeting the Universe. If you take one step towards the Universe, it will take ninety-nine steps towards you.

We are creating our lives, constantly, and more often than not, it is the unconscious that is calling the shots. How can we place more emphasis on the conscious creation when we find ourselves at odds with what we have manifested for ourselves? If you are ready to receive change, look at that thing that is out of alignment and accept that you have created it. Be careful what voice you use when you look at yourself. How does your mind talk to you? Perhaps it says, "I am stupid beyond belief to have created another one of these bad relationships. I am an idiot because I'm about to make the same mistake again." When you catch this kind of negative self-talk, try to contact the unconscious part of you that tells you you're not worthy or loveable. When you start to use that ability (that we all have) to practice self-compassion, you'll see that you don't need to beat yourself up anymore. You begin to consciously eliminate what is no longer useful in your life.

If you find yourself always struggling with finances, relationships or another aspect of your life, somewhere in your subconscious there's probably an internal script running that you're not aware of, saying you're not worthy to have money or love. People repeat destructive patterns in their lives, which are almost always subconscious. It has nothing to do with being unlucky or doomed, and everything to do with something that you are doing or not doing. We radiate out the energy that creates our reality. It may be hard to accept responsibility for your own actions, but YOU are the only one who can truly make your life better. There are reasons why your life may not be what you'd like it to look like. There is help and support out there, but you have to take the journey to arrive at who you really are, and want to be. No one else can take it for you, and no external event or circumstance can guide you to the truth. Your story tells you how you got to where you are, but an abundant view of life is one in which you're not bound by the past. It informs you but doesn't define you. The possibilities are limitless if you allow them to take flight and soar!

Blame and anger stand in the way of abundance. The subconscious mind is like a library. It creates the language of your mind. Every event that has ever happened to you in your life is registered on your subconscious. The majority of people on the planet are being governed not by their conscious mind, but by what lies beneath. Your subconscious mind has all these ideas, thoughts and experiences that can be triggered. When it comes to abundance, your messaging could be saying, "Hey, you're not a worthwhile person unless you've got a big house, a nice car and 2.3 kids." You may very well have heard some variation of that as you grew-up, but if you blame your parents, or your teachers, or advertisers, or our society, you're not going to be able to move toward your own abundance. Change has to start with you.

It is easy to blame. We think about what we needed as children that we didn't receive from a parent, or how a friend betrayed us, or how certain powerful entities in our society have played unfairly, affecting all of us to varying degrees. There is a lot of anger to go around! As hard as it can be, you must stop blaming other people, things and situations. It is draining you of the energy you need to funnel into your own life and zapping your ability to stay positive. There is a place for anger, if it makes an impression about what is acceptable to you, but once you acknowledge it, let it go. It is time for you to take back your power, sit with your own set of circumstances and begin to look at how to create change. What can you do to manifest something for yourself? What can you do to manifest something that will become big enough to share with somebody else?

ELIMINATING WHAT YOU DON'T NEED - WHAT IS TRULY IMPORTANT TO YOU

Have you ever really thought about what you need? The truth is, a body only requires one meal a day, a nourishing meal, to keep it going, to keep it alive. We also need shelter to keep us from getting ill, but that's about it. How much happier would we be if we could reprogram ourselves to just desiring those two objects? That would be your abundance and you might be blissfully happy with what you have, instead of unhappy with what you don't. Can you detach from "things" and embrace a consciousness that rises above materialism? Think about it – lack is the absence of something. When lack and scarcity drive you and set the tone in your life, you are letting the idea of things that don't even exist to rule you. We have to learn now to stop wanting unnecessary clutter in our lives. The pursuit of it, and the pressure we put on ourselves to obtain it is also cluttering our abundance energy. Our culture of "more" is always trying to convince you that you'll be able to fill emptiness with things. How do you genuinely fill a void within? With self-love and giving to others. If your happiness is dependent on external effects, you can see the trouble that you might end up in when it is taken away, can't you? Things come and go, as do people. The only constant is you. What are the things that satisfy you, and make you feel content? Think about the love of family, the gestures of friends, laughter, the time you take to relax, the flower that just bloomed. Look around and stop chasing abstractions. Save your energy for making meaningful connections with the world, taking care of yourself and giving to others. Stop comparing yourself to other people. You don't know what it is like to be anybody else but yourself. Just because someone has more money and possessions doesn't mean they have more abundance.

Unless we look at the basics of what we really need, we're going to suffer on the personal and global level. By embracing the idea of bigger, larger, more lavish, more expensive in our individual lives, and globally, we have allowed ourselves to become disconnected from each other. Do you remember when we would go to the neighbor's for a cup of sugar and kids would go outside after school to play with other kids, not in a cyber world, but on real grass under real trees? We just need to reconnect with each other. Let's embody the truth that we are capable of creating our own world. Can you make your own life less complicated and less full of "stuff," which will help you to live in simple abundance?

I can remember a time when I slept in a bedroom with five brothers with only an army blanket thrown over us. Were we cold? Yes! But we survived. As far as our communication and connection, we were not distracted by all the materialistic things, the technology and all the stuff that keep us entrapped in our own little prisons that we have made for ourselves these days. Abundance is actually about wanting what you have, right now. Not that you can't aspire to change, but if you paint your life in a negative light, you're just going to create more negativity. What might be good within a seemingly negative experience? Is there a seed of truth and reflection in there to be learned when you make do with what you have? Get rid of what you don't need, such as objects or situations that don't fulfill you. If you want to be happy, create happiness, and then you'll attract more of it!

GIVING AND SERVICE – THE WAY TO ABUNDANCE

Life is all about stops and starts. I have never met anyone who was at peace or happy all the time, but there are people who "hold" a lot of peace and happiness. The most content people I've come across are the ones that were helping other people. It wasn't about how much money they were making or material stuff they had in their lives. Helping someone contributes to your self-worth. The next time you're feeling a little bit down or out of sorts, find some service work to do. Service and giving are very powerful parts of the abundance equation. It can be the smallest gesture, like picking up a piece of trash everyday, or tutoring the neighbor's kid in math when the family can't afford paid help. What contributions can you make to someone close to you, a stranger, your community, or to the world? Think about what kinds of service you have done in the past. Tap into the abundance of how giving has made you feel.

Money is energy and energy must flow in order to be effective. When you hold on to money, I guarantee it will make you unhappy. It takes on an unnatural and skewed importance that breeds scarcity mentality. The same is true with extra amounts of whatever you have. You need to do something with it, actively, or the waste becomes a burden. Do you have a lot of time to give? Skills you can share? Love to offer? If you want more abundance in your life, give abundance away! You'll find that it returns to you, ten-fold in some form or another. I make sure that I keep giving, because in giving you receive everything. When you begin to serve other people you actually fulfill your own dreams.

Always be willing to help somebody, because in doing so you're opening up the abundance door. You never know what will come through it, or when you need help at some point in your own life. Be generous of heart, and of spirit, and look at what it is your manifesting. Money is not enough to fix everything. It takes people coming together, communicating, combining their skills and working towards a greater good. We are always in abundance. It is how it is used, where it is directed, and whether it is in the right alignment that makes the difference for both the person giving and the one receiving.

ABUNDANCE AND MINDFULNESS

Mindfulness, the practice of being aware and in the moment, is helpful in all aspects of life. Abundance is a particularly appropriate partner for mindfulness. Keeping your focus on the here and now, and opening up your conscious outlook, are key to living abundantly. We can use mindfulness to address both the bigger picture of remembering all our potential and resilience, and also in the elements of our daily lives. It is a way to keep your thoughts positive and inspire actions that bring you closer to what you want.

There is simplicity to mindfulness that mirrors the pure form of abundance, which is uncluttered and easy. Life is complicated, no doubt, but you have to clear away all the junk that your mind likes to dig up and throw in your way! Ask yourself, "Am I living with purpose, beyond the problems and challenges I may be experiencing?" Can you see over hurdles? Are you passionate about certain things that you can concentrate on when you're weighed down by negative feelings? On practical terms, can you spend more time doing things that don't cost money, that reconnect you with a more balanced life?

Mindfulness puts us in touch with all that we see, feel, hear, taste, and think. Worries about money cause stress and can shut down your senses. Then, your self-care, your sleep, and your eating habits take a nose dive, all making you less able to weather a storm. Worrying about the future, and having regret or shame about the past won't change anything! It is only going to deplete your energy and paralyze you. Living in a mindful state of abundance allows you to have those worries, but not for long. You get back on a forward-looking path. You tackle your challenges calmly and methodically, and avoid becoming overwhelmed. Feel all your feelings but notice when they are spinning and swirling down a dark hole. Be aware of what triggers that sensation and shift your energy. Remember to have gratitude, be in the present and enjoy the journey, wherever it takes you.

So many people have a limited perspective. There may be people around you – family or friends – who feel that it is helpful to tell you that your dreams are impossible. They say it is for your own good and that they are only trying to help because they care about you. Well, thank them then go back to your reality! No one can stomp on your aspirations and goals. If you are authentically you, and you know the truth lies inside, not in your external life, you will be living in abundance.

EXERCISES/MEDITATIONS ON ABUNDANCE

Abundance Meditation

Any kind of meditation can help to center you and give you a stronger, more realistic perspective on abundance, and open you to all its possibilities. Here is a meditation that uses the symbolism of gold to represent the abundance that is available to you, and the theme of sharing it with others.

Find a quiet room or space where you'll be undisturbed for a while. Make yourself comfortable as you sit and take a few deep breaths, knowing that for the next few minutes, no one is expecting anything from you. Your only re-

sponsibility is to allow yourself to relax and enjoy this meditation.

Imagine yourself in a safe and calm environment, perhaps somewhere outside where you feel absolutely secure, happy, and confident. Take another deep breath and exhale. Now imagine yourself holding one of your hands in front of you, palm facing up. In the palm your hand rests a beautiful piece of gold. Feel the weight it. Take note of the richness of its color and the light that it reflects back to you.

Now imagine that this piece of gold is starting to grow and multiply. Right before your eyes, the gold keeps getting bigger. At a certain point the gold is so large, you realize you have to start giving some of it away to others. Notice who you are giving the gold to, and become aware of why you are giving it to them, focusing on the answer. Take another deep breath, exhale, and slowly come back into the room. Open your eyes, and reflect on your experience.

The Abundance Gratitude List

The practice of writing gratitude lists is a wonderful way to remind ourselves of what we have at this very moment, and how we can build on the happiness that appreciation, mindfulness and a positive outlook can bring us. There are many approaches to creating a gratitude list (daily, weekly, for yourself, as something to share, etc.) but finding what works for you can help define what abundance means in *your* life, and prompt you to take nothing for granted.

Writing down what you are grateful for allows you to hold a list in your hands, reflect on it, reread it, and save your thoughts. It can focus you "in the moment" and compel you to think about what you DO have, rather than what you don't have. A list also clarifies what you can give away, because you have so much!

These are some of the topics and areas of life that your Abundance-Gratitude List can touch on:

- Family
- Friends
- Work/Relationships
- Home, Food, Nourishment
- The Environment – From the big (say, a waterfall) to the small (the song of a bird, a warm summer breeze)
- Your strengths… and even your weakness, since you learn from them!
- Kindness – from and to you
- Encouragement, positive feedback, compassion
- Feelings
- Love – in your life, and in the world
- Life/Health
- Your goals and dreams
- Something you have read, heard, or observed
- A smile, a laugh, a gasp of wonder

- Anything! Things about you, things around you, things that the universe shares.

The Simple Way to Simplicity

Creating simplicity in your life can give you a new perspective on abundance, as you see how less can truly be more in so many ways! Though it may seem difficult to pare down our needs and desires, making small changes, and building upon them, can bring considerable improvements to your life. You'll begin to create emotional and spiritual space for the kind of abundance that is lasting and emulates from within.

Try these tips:

- Create a realistic budget and stick to it. Yes, there will be times where the unexpected – and the special occasion – comes up, but commit to work with a framework that relieves stress and worry.

- Organize your chores and errands. Try to shop less frequently. Buy a week's worth of food in one trip to the store.
- Clean and keep tidy as you go along. Leaving things until they are a huge job may seem overwhelming. This goes for any kind of task or work that you have to attend to.
- Stop as you buy things and ask, "do I really need this?"
- Put thought into how you spend your money. Think about how giving to others balances your life.
- Take breaks during your day.
- Let go of some of your commitments. Learn to say "no." Ask yourself how YOU really want to spend your time and energy.
- Own fewer clothes, things, and cars. Donate what you don't need.

Unclutter your life.

- Get enough sleep and exercise. Eat a healthy diet.
- Know when to quit something that isn't working for you.
- Don't let procrastination take on a life of its own. You'll spend more time thinking about how you have to do something, than actually doing it. Often, what seemed like an onerous task or duty turns out to be enjoyable and rewarding!
- Resist the urge to make things in life more complicated than they need to be. Parenting, relationships and jobs can certainly be intricate, but think about how you can downgrade tension and problems. Take a deep breath and fight the temptation to react. Find out what triggers you and avoid these things if you can.
- Know when to ask for help, and help someone else.

ABOUT THE AUTHOR

For more than 15 years, Derek O'Neill has been transforming the lives of thousands of people around the world for the better. An internationally acclaimed transformational coach and therapist, motivational speaker, author, martial arts sensei and humanitarian, Derek inspires and uplifts people from all walks of life through his workshops, consultations, speaking engagements, media, and tireless humanitarian work.

Drawing on thirty years of training in martial arts, which earned him the level of Master Black Belt, coupled with his extraordinary intuitive abilities and expertise as a psychotherapist, Derek has pioneered a new psychology, transformational therapy. His signature process, aptly named "The Sword and the Brush," helps clients to seamlessly transmute their struggles into positive outcomes, using the sword to cut away old patterns and the brush to help paint the picture of the new life that they require.

In addition to reaching large audiences through workshops and media, Derek advises individuals, celebrities, business leaders, and politicians, helping them to find new perspectives on long-standing issues and bringing harmony back to their lives and businesses. Inspired by his worldly travels, he formed SQ Foundation, a not-for-profit organization focused on helping to solve global issues facing humanity today. In 2012, he was honored as Humanitarian of the Year and named International Celebrity Ambassador for Variety International the Children's Charity. He was welcomed as Vice President of the esteemed charity in May 2013.

Author of *More Truth Will Set You Free,* the *Get a Grip* series of pocket books, a cutting edge book on parenting titled *Calm Mama, Happy Baby,* and several children's books, Derek also hosted his own radio show, "The Way With Derek O'Neill," which enjoyed the most successful launch in VoiceAmerica's history, quickly garnering 100,000 listeners.

Derek is a master at offering practical wisdom and proven techniques for living a more harmonious and fulfilling life, bringing CEOs to the level of wise yogi and wise yogis to CEO. Derek has been featured in *Exceptional People Magazine, The Irish Independent, The Irish Examiner,* CBS television, and RTE, Ireland's national TV network.

Recordings of Derek's discourses are available for download, offering practical wisdom and proven techniques for living a more harmonious and fulfilling life.

To learn more about Derek O'Neill, to attend his next workshops, to order books, downloads, video streaming, or to contact him, please visit his website:

www.derekoneill.com

To learn more about Derek's SQ Foundation, the global charity that is changing the lives of hundreds of thousands of people around the world, go to:

www.sq-foundation.org

MORE RESOURCES FROM DEREK O'NEILL

Videos, Audio Downloads, Live Broadcasts, Books, Blog and more at:
www.derekoneill.com

"Get a Grip" Book Series

Happiness - You Must Be Effin' Joking!
Anger – Who Gives a Shite?
Relationships – Would You Want to Date You?
Depression – What's that?
Weight – What's Eating You?
Confidence – Easy for You to Say
Abundance – Starts Right Now
Fear - A Powerful Illusion

Children's Books

Water Drop Coloring Book
The Adventures of Lucinda in Love-Filled Fairyland

SOCIAL MEDIA

Follow on YouTube
www.youtube.com/user/DerekONeill101

Like on Facebook
www.facebook.com/derekoneill101

Follow on Twitter
www.twitter.com/DerekONeill101

Connect on LinkedIn
www.linkedin.com/in/derekoneill101